THE
MEMORIAL
RITUALS BOOK
FOR HEALING
AND HOPE

Edited and Compiled by
Ann Marie Putter

Library of Congress Catalog Number: 96-28349
ISBN: 0-89503-143-4 (Paper)

Library of Congress Cataloging-in-Publication Data

The memorial rituals book for healing and hope / edited and compiled
   by Ann Marie Putter.
        p.   cm.
   Includes bibliographical references.
   ISBN 0-89503-143-4 (pbk.)
     1. Bereavement- -Religious aspects. 2. Rites and ceremonies.
I. Putter, Ann Marie.
BL600.M45 1997
291.3'8- -dc20
                                                        96-28349
                                                          CIP

TO:

Mom and Dad,

and especially Sonny and Yoni
with gratitude for their love and support

and, of course . . . to
Shira . . .
who started it all.

ACKNOWLEDGMENTS

with thanks

To the Families, Friends, and Volunteers of *Children Grieve, Too,*
who have taught me so much.

sincere appreciation to those who read the manuscript and supported my work

Bob Baugher, Ph.D., Sandra Bertman, Ph.D., Lois Dick, M.S.W.,
Mel Erickson, Rabbi Earl Grollman, D.D., Bev Hatter, M.S.W.,
John Morgan, Ph.D., Darcie Sims, Ph.D.,
Judy Tatelbaum, M.S.W., Alan Wolfelt, Ph.D.,
and Barb Zick, M.A.

with special memories of

de Olson who taught me the unique Native-American rituals.

All the Conference Committees and their support in planning
and carrying out the rituals used to help people heal.

The Western Washington Bereavement Specialists and the
Western Washington Kids Network for the
opportunities to create rituals.

a simple and sincere thank you to all of the special gifts in my life who have been loving, supportive, and have helped me grow and heal:

Hanan Berman, Cathy Brannan, Dick Goldsmith, Bev Chappell,
Nanette Freeman, Sharon Grollman, Gerri Haynes, Jane Levite,
Ben Joshua Jaffee, and Steve Overman

Karl and Ellen Zahlis for caring

Earl Grollman for his belief in me and love of spirit

TABLE OF CONTENTS

*Some rituals are repeated because they can be used in a variety of settings.

INTRODUCTION

People involved in the death and dying movement have long known of the importance of memories in the healing of the bereaved. For many, experiential activities are more helpful than words. It is with that in mind that I have compiled a series of rituals that have been successfully used with the bereaved. Much of my experience has been working with groups of parents and children, and working with professionals. There are four parts to any ritual: 1) setting the tone before the activity; 2) the actual ritual often accompanied by words, meditation, or song; 3) concluding the ritual, and finally; 4) processing the ritual.

To *set the tone* you might need to ask the group to form a circle, to all sit in the same area, to stand, or give some general instruction. Often when there are mixed ages, I remind the group that this is a "quiet, thinking time" as the younger children don't understand the need for listening during the activity. All materials for the ritual should have been gathered ahead of time, and once the "tone" is set and the group is ready, you can move directly into the ritual. Many rituals begin with silence and then a reading. Examples of readings are in the latter section of this book.

There are examples of many types of rituals on the following pages. All have been used with groups as well as families and individuals. The *actual ritual* usually involves some readings, passing out of the materials (candles, flowers, seedlings, bottles of bubbles), the people in the group responding to the item they are given by saving the deceased's name, or some appropriate phrase, and *closing the ritual* with a moment of silence, final reading or meditation, or simply a concluding phrase indicating the ritual to be over. Finally, most facilitators and often the clients like to *process* or *discuss the ritual,* and how it felt to them.

There are few opportunities in today's "hurry up and be over it" world that afford the bereaved a safe place to talk about and mention a loved one. Especially one who died some time ago. There are even fewer times the name, personality, or achievements of a dead family member or friend can be said aloud publicly. These rituals give grieving family members a time and place to acknowledge the memories, to tell others of the significance of this person in their lives. Whether in a larger group, as a family, or as an individual, rituals are important and creative ways to help the bereaved to heal.

Ann Marie Putter
April 1996

DEFINITION

rit-u-al

(rich'oo el)

adj. of, like, or done as a rite {ritual sacrifices in ancient religions}

n. 1 a system or form of **rites** in a **religion** / The *ritual* of many
faiths includes Communion./ **2** anything done at regular
intervals, as if it were a **rite** {A 30-minute walk
is one of my daily rituals}.

a **ceremony** means an act that is done according to strict rules and
in a serious way. **Rite** usually refers to a religious ceremony that
has set words and actions. **Ritual** means a group of rites
or ceremonies, frequently of a particular religion.

Webster's Dictionary for Young Adults

RITUALS
AND THEIR IMPORTANCE

Ritual is defined as a ceremony or body of ceremonies repeated routinely. It is also seen as a social gesture. There are five fundamental human needs that ritual meets:

1. To establish order
- functions on socially agreed-upon automatic pilot
- to create a sameness and familiarity
- all ritualization is about the ordering of experience

2. To reaffirm meaning
- all rituals communicate meaning
- affirm the central meaning-structure of the community
- face questions of life and death, love and evil, the origin and destiny of the human race and universe

3. To bond community
- shared symbols and shared actions bond a community through both the appearance and the experience of acting as one
- communities to which we belong supply us with the cognitive home of a shared world view, and the emotional home of people who will recognize, support, and accept us.

4. To handle ambivalence (sense of opposite or conflict)
- provide a safe mode of expression of conflicting emotions
- ritual should not assign feeling, but it can allow symbolic room for feelings

5. To encounter mystery
- place of encountering the luminous, spiritual, transcendent
- to beckon the power of the almighty

Handout from Jim Christiansen

* * * * * * * * * * * * * * * * * * *

HOLIDAY RITUALS

* * * * * * * * * * * * * * * * * * *

NAME OF RITUAL
Beginning the Year

USED FOR
To start grief/bereavement groups

APPROPRIATE AGES
Four and up

LENGTH OF TIME
Fifteen to twenty minutes

MATERIALS NEEDED
Everyone uses their names for this activity

DESCRIPTION
Early in group all the children receive a name tag with their names in large block letters. A game is played asking questions about the names, who has the longest, shortest name; the name with the most vowels, who has a name with a "y" in it, etc. As many questions as possible are asked, and then all name tags are put away and people try to remember each other's names and who died.

NAME OF RITUAL

Hearts and Band-Aids or Hearts and Mini-Gold Safety Pins

USED FOR

Valentine's Day during February

APPROPRIATE AGES

All

LENGTH OF TIME

Twenty minutes

MATERIALS NEEDED

Enough foil wrapped hearts or Hershey kisses and tiny band-aids for all participants. A container to pass these things. If gold-pins are used, a small container to pass these.

DESCRIPTION

Form a circle of participants. Facilitator talks about this special time of the year when our thoughts turn to the love in our hearts. Speak of how we have feelings of love all the time, but in February it feels a little easier to speak of love because society acknowledges it with Valentine's Day. Speak of the part of our heart that needs to heal and how we form a sore and sometimes cover sores with band-aids. Speak of the sweetness in our hearts for the beloved, whether they are here or have died. Ask everyone present to take a heart (the wholeness and sweetness) and a band-aid (the pain and sore that is healing within the whole). When each person takes their heart and band-aid they are invited to say the name or something loving about the deceased. If a gold pin is used instead of a band-aid, the pin reminds you of the sore or pain that will always be in the heart, but the love that helps to heal it.

NAME OF RITUAL
Memorial Valentines

USED FOR
Valentine Activity Day and Groups that fall during February

APPROPRIATE AGES
All

LENGTH OF TIME
About one hour to prepare

MATERIALS NEEDED
Red, white, and pink construction paper, stickers, yarn, lace doilies, glue, scissors, tissue paper, contact paper, popsicle sticks

DESCRIPTION
Families/participants make heart shaped valentines and decorate them as they wish. On the back of the valentines they write a message to the deceased including the name and dates of the deceased. They also include the date this was made. Then they cover the valentine(s) with contact paper and can add the popsicle sticks so that the valentine can be taken to the cemetery and will stay in the ground. If there is no close cemetery or the person wasn't buried, a plant can be bought and planted at the home and the valentine placed in the plant or the dirt.

NAME OF RITUAL

Egg Rituals—eggs symbolize rebirth as well as the continuing life cycle. Eggs have no beginnings or endings.

USED FOR

Easter and Passover

APPROPRIATE AGES

Six and up

LENGTH OF TIME

Forty-five minutes to make it; fifteen minutes to share it

MATERIALS NEEDED

Paper, crayons, markers, scissors, stickers, ribbon, felt, hole punch, plastic "egg shaped" eggs, basket with foil-wrapped miniature eggs to share

DESCRIPTION

Similar to Memorial ornaments, plastic eggs are used to hold special memories or gifts. A message on paper can be placed inside the egg which would list the deceased person's dates or a special thought about Easter or Passover. The outside of the egg is decorated with art items, and a ribbon or yarn is attached to be able to hang the egg from somewhere around the house or taken to the cemetery. If appropriate, the egg can serve as part of the centerpiece for the holiday.

NAME OF RITUAL
Mother's Day/Father's Day Rituals

USED FOR
Helping with the difficult days when there is no longer a mother/father or parents

APPROPRIATE AGES
Five and up

LENGTH OF TIME
About fifty minutes for the activity and fifteen to twenty minutes for sharing

MATERIALS NEEDED
Crayons, markers, paper, stickers, poems, pens, pencils, ribbons, fabric, scissors, glue, yarn, clear contact paper

DESCRIPTION
Families are asked to fold paper in half to create a card. Using markers, stickers, etc. a message is sent to the deceased on the card and the card(s) are decorated appropriately. When completed the cards are covered with clear contact paper so they can be exposed to the weather. Then the families stand in a circle and share a special memory of the parent. This can be combined with a planting ceremony as well.

NAME OF RITUAL

"Bubbles"

USED FOR

Outside activity day, "Anger" activity

APPROPRIATE AGES

All

LENGTH OF TIME

This can be a short or lengthy activity depending on how it is framed and the purpose of the activity

MATERIALS NEEDED

Small bottles of soapy bubble water, ideally one per child, or one per family

DESCRIPTION

The idea behind bubble activities is to "blow" away or let go of difficult feelings. This is especially nice to do with youngsters at camp where the bubbles are fun to chase. Bubble activities are appropriate for discussion about the kinds of feelings we hold inside and how helpful it is to blow out, or let go of difficult feelings. When the children let the bubbles go it is good to help them articulate something they are letting go of, e.g., anger, sadness, pain. Naturally, the children get to take the bottles of bubbles with them at the close of the activity.

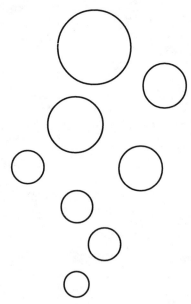

NAME OF RITUAL
　　Fall Leaves

USED FOR
　　September/October activity

APPROPRIATE AGES
　　Four and up

LENGTH OF TIME
　　Fifteen minutes

MATERIALS NEEDED
　　Fall leaves of many colors, a basket to place them in. If leaves are hard to get, craft stores have "silk" fall leaves which are very realistic and nice because they last.

DESCRIPTION
　　Ritual should be proceeded by either the story *Freddy the Leaf* by Buscalia, or a discussion of leaves and their colors and their cycle of life. After forming a circle, everyone is invited to take a leaf that "speaks" to them and then metaphorically telling how this leaf is like the deceased: it is long (tall), it likes lots of colors, it is a little wrinkled, it is falling apart, etc. Everyone goes around the circle telling the specialness of the leaf (deceased) and then closes the ritual with a "hand hug" (see page 36).

NAME OF RITUAL
Halloween Feeling Masks

USED FOR
Halloween Activity Day, October group activity

APPROPRIATE AGES
All

LENGTH OF TIME
Thirty to forty-five minutes for making; fifteen minutes for circle sharing

MATERIALS NEEDED
Paper plates, felt or material, sequins, crayons, markers, yarn, ribbons, scissors, glue, colored paper, buttons, etc.

DESCRIPTION
Children decide which feeling they wish to portray on their masks. They create a face that displays that feeling using any of the above art materials. On the "inside" of the mask they can write what feeling they are acknowledging and why. During the sharing part of the ritual they wear their mask and participants try to guess the feeling. When all have participated they go around the circle and talk about Halloween without the loved one.

NAME OF RITUAL
Christmas/Hanukkah Memorial Ornaments

USED FOR
December Activity Day

APPROPRIATE AGES
Four and up

LENGTH OF TIME
About forty-five minutes to make, about twenty minutes for ritual

MATERIALS NEEDED
Hollow plastic circular or diamond shaped ornaments; fabric paints, usually red, green, gold, and silver; ivory colored parchment paper; markers, crayons, colored pencils; scissors; glue stick or tape. Hershey red, silver, and green foil wrapped candy. Ribbon to attach ornament to tree or other special place. Clothesline or similar cord to hang the ornaments from while they are painted and drying.

DESCRIPTION
Have families each choose an ornament; take a piece of parchment paper and write a message to the deceased with a special Christmas or Hanukkah wish for themselves and the deceased. Decorate the paper in any way they want and then roll or fold the message into the ornament. Put two or three chocolate kisses into the plastic ornament and then close and glue the two parts together. With the ribbon or ornament hook, hang the ornament from a string so that it is hanging free. Now apply the fabric paint in whatever way you might want. Stickers or other fabric pieces can also be used. Somewhere on the ornament put the date, e.g., "1996" and when finished allow this to dry.

NAME OF RITUAL
Candle Ceremonies

USED FOR
Closing groups; December holiday
activities; Campfires

APPROPRIATE AGES
Candles are appropriate for all ages,
but if the ritual requires holding
of hot candles, parents should be
holding (or helping to hold)
candles for all children under ten

LENGTH OF TIME
As long as it takes to go around the circle, about twenty minutes

MATERIALS NEEDED
Candles, candle holders (paper discs that are placed on the base of
the candle to prevent wax from dripping on the hand). If you are
making the candles you need beeswax in sheets, the wick,
scissors, rulers, etc.

DESCRIPTION
There are many ways to use candles in ceremonies and rituals.
Our fall and winter groups (10-week closed groups) frequently end
with lighting candles. We use Sabbath candles sold in Jewish
bookstores. These are a uniform size, do not usually drip, and are
small, but easy to grip. We have used tea candles and votives, but
both of these are small and need to be placed on a table, whereas
the Sabbath candles can be held quite easily. A circle is formed,
either around a campfire, a table or around the room. A large
center candle is lit by a match and then the facilitator might
choose to speak of the healing of light, the spirit of the group
embodied in the candle, the warmth of help found in the group
(see readings at end of book). Following this talk the facilitator
will light his/her candle from the large one and say the name of
the deceased; then the facilitator lights the candle next to him/her
and that person says the name and so on throughout the circle. If
this is done inside it is helpful to lower the lights. Candle ceremonies are usually very powerful experiences, and blowing out
the candle can be difficult. Participants are asked to blow out the
candle "when they are ready" and usually the sharing of food
following the ceremony is helpful to give people time to "put
themselves together" again.

* * * * * * * * * * * * * * * * * * *

CAMP RITUALS

* * * * * * * * * * * * * * * * * * *

NAME OF RITUAL
Name Rituals

USED FOR
Bonding the group, this is usually used at camp and Activity Day

APPROPRIATE AGES
All

LENGTH OF TIME
Goes quickly, only a few minutes

MATERIALS NEEDED
Voices

DESCRIPTION
The idea here is to allow safety and comfort to develop with the group as they say the name of the deceased. If this is done in a group the suggestion is to form a circle at the beginning of the day and have everyone whisper the name of the person. About halfway through the day, the group asks everyone to quickly form a circle and say the name at a natural pitch. At least one more time before the end of group everyone again forms a circle and says the name a little louder. Finally at the close of group a circle is formed and the name is shouted out! If this is done at camp the circles are formed on Friday and Saturday evenings with the final circle done at the close of camp with everyone shouting the name.

NAME OF RITUAL

Solstice

USED FOR

Camp or Activity Day

APPROPRIATE AGES

Six and up

LENGTH OF TIME

This ritual is created individually and then the group places these on bushes, trees and plants during a nature walk, so the group part is about as long as the walk takes.

MATERIALS NEEDED

Large green circles with smaller yellow circles; the circles have been glued inside of each other; a yellow or green piece of yarn has been put through a punched hole at the top of the solstice. These can all be prepared ahead of time and handed out the day the ritual is to be completed.

DESCRIPTION

The children (families) are given the solstice and invited to send a message to the deceased by writing a note or drawing a picture on the solstice. The message can be as simple as "I miss you" or as lengthy as a poem or phrase of love. Younger children might want to draw a picture. When completed, the group takes a nature walk and while wandering through the trees finds a place to hang the solstice. Another option is to walk to a nearby cemetery (or take it to the cemetery where the deceased is) and leave it. The solstice can always be completed during the group activity and then taken home and attached to a tree or plant in the garden.

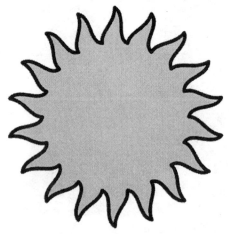

NAME OF RITUAL
Pine Cones at the Fireside

USED FOR
Campfire activity after a sing-a-long

APPROPRIATE AGES
Ten and up

LENGTH OF TIME
As long as it takes the group to share, giving each person about three minutes

MATERIALS NEEDED
Pine cones or some type of cone found during nature walks at camp

DESCRIPTION
Each participant comes to the campfire with two or three cones. They are told to look for these pine cones the day of the campfire. Once they are at the campfire a primary facilitator will model what it is that they should do. This is another "letting go" ritual. The participants will "let go" of their anger at the deceased for dying by throwing their anger out and allowing it to "burn" up. One pine cone is thrown into the fire. Then the participants might let go of their guilt over something; another participant will let go of their fear of the death; still another might let go of their sadness at not being there when the death occurred. With each "letting go" a pine cone is tossed into the fire. This can be a very cathartic ritual, but obviously a highly emotional one. While the pine cones and fire make it a camp ritual, another option would be to put each "letting go" onto a piece of paper and "throw them out" in the garbage, or into a paper bag that could be burned.

NAME OF RITUAL
Hands

USED FOR
Closing of camp weekend

APPROPRIATE AGES
All, although young children may need help in tracing their hand

LENGTH OF TIME
Varies; this can be done over several days (like at a camp weekend), or within a thirty-minute period

MATERIALS NEEDED
Light colored construction paper, pencils, crayons, markers, scissors, felt scraps, ribbon, yarn, large tag board on stand

DESCRIPTION
Participants are asked to trace their hand(s) on construction paper and cut them out. On the inside of the hand a message can be written to the deceased; dates, a poem, etc. On the outside the hand is decorated to look similar to the participant's with rings, nail polish, etc. When the hand(s) are completed they are placed on the tag board along with other hands, all saying "good bye" to the deceased.

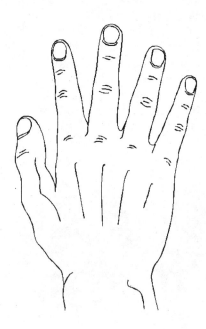

NAME OF RITUAL
Floral Wreath

USED FOR
Camp

APPROPRIATE AGES
All

LENGTH OF TIME
Throughout the weekend; the actual ritual takes about thirty minutes

MATERIALS NEEDED
Grapevine wreath in circular or heart shape, flowers (usually white carnations), pre-cut pieces of paper with a hole punch on the top. All items must be biodegradable.

DESCRIPTION
This special ritual calls for participation of the entire family. The wreath is brought to camp and mounted on an easel or some place in easy reach of everyone. Next to it are the pieces of paper. Everyone is invited to take a piece of paper at some time during the weekend and put a message on it. It can be as simple as the name and dates, or as involved as a poem or letter. This is kept until the "wreath ritual." At the time of the ritual everyone forms a large circle with the wreath held in the middle by one of the facilitators. The facilitator may speak for a moment about nature and returning to the earth. It is helpful to comment on how everything about the wreath is natural, and that both living and dying are natural beginnings and endings. Then, family by family, each come forward and take a flower, place the message on the stem of the flower (through the hole punch) and then weave the flower onto the wreath. Eventually with all families participating, the wreath disappears and only flowers are seen. Further comments on the beauty we carry with us, both "inside" and "out" helps make the symbolism of the ceremony special. When all the families have completed placing their messages and flowers, the entire group walks together to the edge of the water. If possible someone takes the wreath out to the middle of the water (in our case we have the director of the camp). The wreath is taken by boat out to the middle of a body of water and placed where it will float into the ocean.

NAME OF RITUAL

Candle Ceremonies

USED FOR

Closing groups; December holiday activities; Campfires

APPROPRIATE AGES

Candles are appropriate for all ages, but if the ritual requires holding of hot candles, parents should be holding (or helping to hold) candles for all children under ten.

LENGTH OF TIME

As long as it takes to go around the circle, about twenty minutes

MATERIALS NEEDED

Candles, candle holders (paper discs that are placed on the base of the candle to prevent wax from dripping on the hand). If you are making the candles you need beeswax in sheets, the wick, scissors, rulers, etc.

DESCRIPTION

There are many ways to use candles in ceremonies and rituals. Our fall and winter groups (10-week closed groups) frequently end with lighting candles. We use Sabbath candles sold in Jewish bookstores. These are a uniform size, do not usually drip, and are small, but easy to grip. We have used tea candles and votives, but both of these are small and need to be placed on a table, whereas the Sabbath candles can be held quite easily. A circle is formed, either around a campfire, a table or around the room. A large center candle is lit by a match and then the facilitator might choose to speak of the healing of light, the spirit of the group embodied in the candle, the warmth of help found in the group (see readings at end of book). Following this talk the facilitator will light his/her candle from the large one and say the name of the deceased; then the facilitator lights the candle next to him/her and that person says the name and so on throughout the circle. If this is done inside it is helpful to lower the lights. Candle ceremonies are usually very powerful experiences, and blowing out the candle can be difficult. Participants are asked to blow out the candle "when they are ready" and usually the sharing of food following the ceremony is helpful to give people time to "put themselves together" again.

NAME OF RITUAL
Rock Rituals

USED FOR
Closing of group; Camp weekend

APPROPRIATE AGES
All

LENGTH OF TIME
Twenty minutes

MATERIALS NEEDED
Either pre-chosen rocks for a group, or at camp families search for a rock that "speaks" to them. If this is the closing for a group, polished stones are usually provided. One particularly nice stone can be found in Asian stores, a smooth black stone (frequently used in Japanese gardens). The stone is primarily smooth, but there is a rough piece somewhere on it. The idea behind the stones is to find the rough among the smooth.

DESCRIPTION
The group forms a circle and the facilitator asks for quiet to help center the group. The facilitator then talks to the group about healing and hope. The talk centers around how there will always be a piece of them that is rough and raw, that piece that holds the love and memories of the deceased. The talk also focuses on the new strengths the person has gained from the grief they have experienced. Appropriate poems can be said and then (in the group closing) a basket of stones is passed around and everyone takes one and finds the smooth and rough parts. As the rocks are passed and chosen, the participants are invited to say the name of the person that created the rough part of them (the deceased). If this is a camp ritual, frequently the rock found is placed at the bottom of the tree that is planted to give it a sturdy foundation. (See planting of trees.) That way a special part of the family that came to camp stays at camp.

NAME OF RITUAL
Seedlings or Small Flowering Plants

USED FOR
Closing of groups Spring Activity Days; Summer camp activity

APPROPRIATE AGES
All

LENGTH OF TIME
Depends on whether seedlings or plants are passed out, or planted during the ritual

MATERIALS NEEDED
Tree or plant seedlings (as many as there are families), paper messages attached to seedlings or plants, shovels, contact paper, and scissors

DESCRIPTION
Children create a message with pens, paper, and other art materials, being sure to include date on the message. The facilitators then put the message on clear contact paper and punch a hole through the message to tie it to the plant. Children and parents form a circle around the room, or around the planting area, whichever works best. Facilitator talks about nature and seasons, beginnings and endings. Each family is given a seedling/plant and attaches their message to it. The group usually says a poem to close the ceremony.

NAME OF RITUAL
Native-American Rope Ritual

USED FOR
Closings, at camp and end of groups,
frequently used to end a training event

APPROPRIATE AGES
All, although younger children won't
understand the symbolism of this activity

LENGTH OF TIME
Depends on number participating

MATERIALS NEEDED
Macrame white or off white rope, large enough to make a full circle of the group with all standing outside the rope, scissors able to easily cut rope

DESCRIPTION
The rope ritual is a favorite of *Children Grieve, Too*, families and facilitators. A lengthy rope is brought to the room or location of the group at the beginning of the event (group, training, camp weekend). Whenever rituals are done throughout the activities, everyone stands behind the rope, picks it up and holds it (or ties it together) to form the wholeness of the group. At camp, for example, the Friday evening of the weekend everyone gathers around the edge of the room and the rope is passed out and held in front of them, tying the two ends together to form a circle. Again Saturday morning and evening the day begins and ends with everyone standing outside the rope and saying some appro-priate thing about wholeness and caring. To close the weekend on Sunday everyone gathers outside the rope (which has symbolized the wholeness and healing we have gotten from each other and the camp). The rope is then untied where it was joined on Friday night, and each person cuts off a small portion of the rope to take that wholeness and spirit with them. To do the cutting, a knot is placed in the rope (carrying the specialness inside the knot), and then the rope is cut right after the knot. Frequently the name of the deceased is mentioned when tying the knot, or some feeling that has been gained by being together for the group or weekend, e.g., "I carry with me the strength," "I carry with me the love," "I carry with me the hope, etc." This is a special activity because the families acknowledge their connection and had the death not occurred, they would not have met.

NAME OF RITUAL
   Planting of Trees

USED FOR
   Closing Ceremonies at Camp

APPROPRIATE AGES
   Four and up

LENGTH OF TIME
   Thirty to forty minutes

MATERIALS NEEDED
   Flowering tree, fertilizer, hole (already dug if possible), shovel(s), water, rocks to place in hole

DESCRIPTION
   The final ritual at our weekend camp is the planting of a flowering tree in memory of all who died. The camp graciously digs the hole before we come to the ceremony. During the two days at camp everyone is asked to find a rock, flower, shell, or something that "speaks" to them to add to the plant. At the time of the ceremony everyone forms a circle around the hole. The facilitator models what we ask of the families. She/he stands at the center of the circle next to the hole and speaks about growth that has come from the weekend, spirit and beauty that has come from each other, wonder and excitement about the new things learned at camp, love of and for the deceased. At this point the entire group reads a poem responsively (see prayers, poems at the end of this book). Then the facilitator places a stone or something in the hole next to the tree and says "I place this _____ in memory of _____, my (father, mother, sister, brother) and to help this tree grow (strong, beautiful, lively, happy, etc.). Each person in turn goes to the tree and places something in memory of someone and to help the tree. When all have done this, the fertilizer is placed in the hole on the roots of the plant. Then the facilitator models putting some dirt over the roots, and again, each person that wishes, places some dirt with the shovel over the plant. Then the plant is watered and the circle comes together in a hand hug.

NAME OF RITUAL
Native-American Burden Basket

USED FOR
Camp and Conferences

APPROPRIATE AGES
Anyone old enough to write a
message or find something
special to place in the basket

LENGTH OF TIME
Any time is appropriate as this
is done individually

MATERIALS NEEDED
Native-American basket placed on a small table which is usually
covered with a Native-American blanket and some cedar boughs.
Optional: a picture of Mt. Rainier or some nearby mountain
peaks. Pieces of paper, pens, tissue. Frequently candles are used
to decorate the room.

DESCRIPTION
In 1989, a Native-American Shaman made a cedar Burden Basket
for the Seattle Chapter of The Compassionate Friends. Since that
time it has become a tradition to incorporate this ritual into all
Bereavement Services activities. The basket is medium sized and
because it is cedar it is "strong" enough to hold anger and tears.
Families are encouraged to enter the room where the basket is
kept (Reflection Room) and write a note, place a leaf or stone, put
a newspaper article, etc. into the basket. At the close of the
conference all the messages are taken to a Native American who
gives praise and blessing to these items, and then burns them. He
gathers the ashes together and then carries them up to the top of
Mt. Rainier where they are scattered and returned to Mother
Earth. This has been and continues to be a very powerful healing
tool, and of course no one knows what has been placed in the
basket, but it is clear that we are "rid" of the anger and pain and
more open to the healing. Lots of tears are shed in this room. This
can be a very helpful ritual.

* *

GROUP CLOSING
CEREMONIES

* *

NAME OF RITUAL
Balloon Lift-Off

USED FOR
To acknowledge the ending of a group

APPROPRIATE AGES
All, but younger children have difficulty letting a balloon go, so you might need extras

LENGTH OF TIME
The children prepare the balloons, then there is a short ceremony, and then the balloons are let go, so approximately thirty to forty-five minutes

MATERIALS NEEDED
Biodegradable balloons, yarn string, small paper notes to attach to the balloon string

DESCRIPTION
Currently it has been less popular to let balloons "go" due to environmental concerns, but with balloons that degrade, this is still a popular closing ritual. The children/families write a message to the deceased. The front of the message tells the name, dates, and a short phrase of love; the back of the message is preprinted stating the reason the balloon was sent aloft: "If found this balloon was sent up on _____ in memory of my beloved _____ who died on _____. Please handle with love." Once the messages are completed they are attached to the yarn and the group forms a circle. After appropriate messages of hope, each person is invited to let their balloon go. It is important NOT to let these go in a forest or near wires where they can get caught on something.

NAME OF RITUAL
Hand Hugs

USED FOR
Beginning and ending groups, Camp Activities and Activity Days

APPROPRIATE AGES
All

LENGTH OF TIME
Very quick!

MATERIALS NEEDED
Hands

DESCRIPTION
Group is in a circle, either during group or at the end of an activity. Everyone joins hands and the primary facilitator will suggest that we pass a GENTLE hug to each other. A reminder is needed that this is a gentle "hug" not a "squeeze for all you're worth" hug. These are nice to end groups with, or to help kids re-connect after a particularly difficult time. Hand hugs are helpful at the time anger or sadness is expressed.

NAME OF RITUAL
"Bubbles"

USED FOR
Outside activity day, "Anger" activity

APPROPRIATE AGES
All

LENGTH OF TIME
This can be a short or lengthy activity depending on how it is framed and the purpose of the activity

MATERIALS NEEDED
Small bottles of soapy bubble water, ideally one per child, or one per family

DESCRIPTION
The idea behind bubble activities is to "blow" away or let go of difficult feelings. This is especially nice to do with youngsters at camp where the bubbles are fun to chase. Bubble activities are appropriate for discussion about the kinds of feelings we hold inside and how helpful it is to blow out, or let go of difficult feelings. When the children let the bubbles go it is good to help them articulate something they are letting go of, e.g., anger, sadness, pain. Naturally, the children get to take the bottles of bubbles with them at the close of the activity.

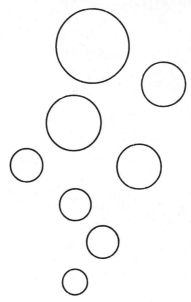

NAME OF RITUAL
Rainbows

USED FOR
Group activity camp ceremony

APPROPRIATE AGES
All

LENGTH OF TIME
Ninety minutes or time over several days

MATERIALS NEEDED
Large blue sheet (mural size) taped to a wall, pre-drawn rainbow on the sheet, colored tissue paper in primary colors, glue sticks, scissors

DESCRIPTION
Children take small colored tissue paper and fold pieces together so they appear crinkled. Glue all of one color in space on the rainbow (all red in top part of the rainbow, all blue, yellow, green, etc.) together so the rainbow becomes 3-D. Over several days, or hours the rainbow takes on a more realistic picture. Once the rainbow is completed form a circle in front of it and talk about how rainbows come from the rain and the sun and speak of the metaphors about healing, sunlight (life), rain, sadness, and how all these things form to make something special, whole, and beautiful.

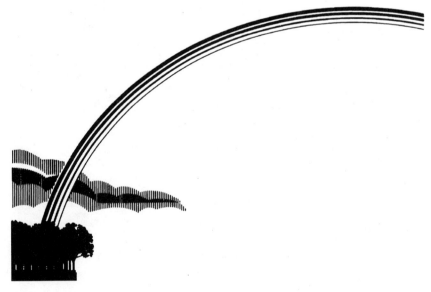

NAME OF RITUAL
Peanuts and Baby Roses

USED FOR
Closing of a group Activity
Day closure

APPROPRIATE AGES
Teens and Adults

LENGTH OF TIME
Twenty minutes

MATERIALS NEEDED
Peanuts in shells, enough for all participants and individual baby roses for each participant. Bowl or something to place these items in while they are taken.

DESCRIPTION
The group should be in a circle. Discussion should center around inside and outside feelings. Sometimes we have a tough outer shell but inside is something special and sweet. All of our outsides are a little different, like the peanut shell, but usually the inside holds a surprise. After encouraging everyone to take a peanut, pass out the rosebuds and again speak about the beauty inside, how we don't always know when or where that beauty will come from, and how special it is when we find it. Everyone takes home the peanut and the rosebud and thinks about the specialness we all have inside which is frequently not visible.

NAME OF RITUAL
Journaling

USED FOR
Acknowledging feelings with youngsters in groups

APPROPRIATE AGES
Teen Groups

MATERIALS NEEDED
Notebooks, paper, pencils, crayons, markers

DESCRIPTION
All are encouraged to acknowledge their feelings with words or pictures. They are told this is a very personal way of sharing feelings, and that there is no "right" or "wrong" way of expressing oneself. The journals may be bought notebooks or created by designing a cover and putting paper (stapling or sewing with yarn) in it. Examples of poetry or drawings are shown, and then the close of each group is a journaling activity. Youngsters are invited to journal or draw about things that came up for them in group, during their week, or just add something special they came across. Journaling is very helpful to many, and there is no one way to do it, giving each participant lots of opportunity to create what they need.

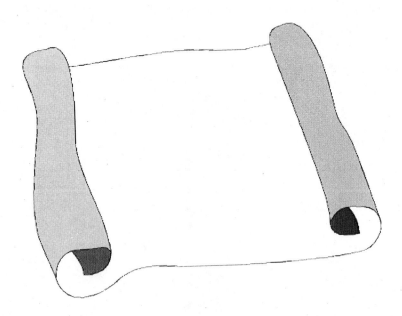

NAME OF RITUAL
Creating Books

USED FOR
Closing of *Children Grieve, Too*, groups each week

APPROPRIATE AGES
All, although for the youngest participants the questions are sometimes changed

MATERIALS NEEDED
During the ten weeks of group the facilitator uses a preformatted page with the children's names listed in alphabetical order. Each week a different question is put on the top of the sheet with the date. When the book is prepared the easiest materials are rainbow colored paper and a simple computer publishing program.

DESCRIPTION
Each week the group "closes" with a final question, i.e., the first night is usually "I came to CGT tonight expecting _____ and it was _____." The second week of group the question usually is "My parent's/sibling's favorite color was and my favorite/brave color is." There are nine questions in all (the 10th week is the closing ceremony). At the end of the nine weeks all the material is formatted into a program with appropriate graphics (i.e., butterflies, rainbows, mountains). The first page of the book tells where and when it occurred and who facilitated, the inside cover tells the first names of the children, their age, who died and cause of death; then follows the pages of the book that the children created. It serves as an important memorial for all the children and a good means for the parents to see how their child answered questions compared to another child with a similar loss. Please see below for usual questions that form the book.

1. I came tonight expecting _____ and it was _____.
2. My parent's favorite color was _____ and my favorite brave color is _____.
3. The change that has happened since my _____ died is _____.
4. Something I remember from the day of the funeral, memorial service is _____.
5. A treasured memory is _____.
6. Something silly/funny I remember doing with my parent is _____.
7. When I miss my _____ I like to _____ to feel better _____.
8. The change that has happened to me since my loved one died is _____ or _____. The change that I think will happen to me in the future is _____.
9. *Children Grieve, Too*, has helped me _____.

NAME OF RITUAL

Seedlings or Small Flowering Plants

USED FOR

Closing of groups; Spring Activity Days; Summer camp activity

APPROPRIATE AGES

All

LENGTH OF TIME

Depends on whether seedlings, plants are passed out, or planted during ritual

MATERIALS NEEDED

Tree or plant seedlings (as many as there are families), paper messages attached to seedlings or plants, shovels, contact paper, and scissors

DESCRIPTION

Children create a message with pens, paper, and other art materials, being sure to include the date on the page. The facilitators then put the message on clear contact paper and punch a hole through the message to tie it to the plant. Children and parents form a circle around the room, or around the planting area, whichever works best. Facilitator talks about nature and seasons, beginnings and endings. Each family is given a seedling/plant and attaches their message to it. The group usually says a poem to close the ceremony.

NAME OF RITUAL
Rock Rituals

USED FOR
Closing of group; Camp weekend

APPROPRIATE AGES
All

LENGTH OF TIME
Twenty minutes

MATERIALS NEEDED
Either pre-chosen rocks for a group, or at camp families search for a rock that "speaks" to them. If this is the closing for a group, polished stones are usually provided. One particularly nice stone can be found in Asian stores, a smooth black stone (frequently used in Japanese gardens). The stone is primarily smooth, but there is a rough piece somewhere on it. The idea behind the stones is to find the rough among the smooth.

DESCRIPTION
The group forms a circle and the facilitator asks for quiet to help center the group. The facilitator then talks to the group about healing and hope. The talk centers around how there will always be a piece of them that is rough and raw, that piece that holds the love and memories of the deceased. The talk also focuses on the new strengths the person has gained from the grief they have experienced. Appropriate poems can be said and then (in the group closing) a basket of stones is passed around and everyone takes one and finds the smooth and rough parts. As the rocks are passed and chosen, the participants are invited to say the name of the person that created the rough part of them (the deceased). If this is a camp ritual, frequently the rock found is placed at the bottom of the tree that is planted to give it a sturdy foundation. (See planting of trees.) That way a special part of the family that came to camp stays at camp.

NAME OF RITUAL

Candle Ceremonies

USED FOR

Closing groups; December holiday
activities; Campfires

APPROPRIATE AGES

Candles are appropriate for all ages,
but if the ritual requires holding
of hot candles, parents should be
holding (or helping to hold)
candles for all children under ten.

LENGTH OF TIME

As long as it takes to go around the circle, about twenty minutes

MATERIALS NEEDED

Candles, candle holders (paper discs that are placed on the base of
the candle to prevent wax from dripping on the hand). If you are
making the candles you need beeswax in sheets, the wick,
scissors, rulers, etc.

DESCRIPTION

There are many ways to use candles in ceremonies and rituals.
Our fall and winter groups (10-week closed groups) frequently end
with lighting candles. We use Sabbath candles sold in Jewish
bookstores. These are a uniform size, do not usually drip, and are
small, but easy to grip. We have used tea candles and votives, but
both of these are small and need to be placed on a table, whereas
the Sabbath candles can be held quite easily. A circle is formed,
either around a campfire, a table or around the room. A large
center candle is lit by a match and then the facilitator might
choose to speak of the healing of light, the spirit of the group
embodied in the candle, the warmth of help found in the group
(see readings at end of book). Following this talk the facilitator
will light his/her candle from the large one and say the name of
the deceased; then the facilitator lights the candle next to him/her
and that person says the name and so on throughout the circle. If
this is done inside it is helpful to lower the lights. Candle ceremonies are usually very powerful experiences, and blowing out
the candle can be difficult. Participants are asked to blow out the
candle "when they are ready" and usually the sharing of food
following the ceremony is helpful to give people time to "put
themselves together" again.

NAME OF RITUAL
Rose Petals: Closing Ritual

USED FOR
Group or camp closings

APPROPRIATE AGES
All

LENGTH OF TIME
Ten to fifteen minutes

MATERIALS NEEDED
One or two fresh roses

DESCRIPTION
At the end of group, a rose is passed around. As each person receives the rose she or he takes a petal in honor of the person who died to acknowledge his/her healing journey. When this ritual is introduced, the person explaining it may refer to the rose as symbolizing love and beauty, the thorns as challenges, etc.

NAME OF RITUAL
Pouch/Stones

USED FOR
Closing of groups

APPROPRIATE AGES
Five to eighteen years old

MATERIALS NEEDED
Eight-inch squares of velvet or felt, ribbon, yarn, laces for drawstring, beads or stones

DESCRIPTION
This is a very flexible activity and can be adapted to a variety of uses. It originated as a way to validate the meaning of loss to the individual child in the context of family (see "Family Circle"). It has been used with beads as a closing ritual for each group session, with each child choosing a bead to represent something relevant from that particular session (i.e., my mad feelings, my dreams about daddy, etc.). One group chose to make bracelets from their beads at the end of their series. Some children have worn their pouches around their neck as a way of holding memories close.

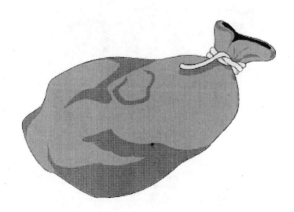

FAMILY CIRCLE
(can be part of previous ritual)

I began, as part of a family circle. My family was not a perfect circle, but a human one, maybe even a little ragged around the edges. My velvet pouch began the same way. As I touch the velvet, I will try to remember what was warm and soft and happy about my family circle.

Then there was death. Like the olden string, death made holes in my world and brought a close to the family circle as it was. Death comes to all living things and is final on earth but death can be used to create something new for me and have a purpose.

My circle of velvet and my string have come together to make a pouch that is useful and beautiful. As I hold it and then empty what is inside, I will try to think about how my death experience can serve a purpose in my life. Can it make me stronger and more independent? Can it help me to help another? What do I hold inside?

Stone #1 tells me to retell the story of death to someone. How did my special someone die? When? Do I remember the first moment someone told me and I understood that my someone had died? What did it feel like when I first understood?

Stone #2 stands for my feelings of missingness, the sad emptiness that lets me know someone is now different. I may cry again. It may help to look at pictures, tell a funny story, draw or write a letter, pray or visit the cemetery. With whatever I feel inside, it is important to DO something to help. It's okay to hurt as long as I need to, but then I will be ready to move on. I say good-bye.

Stone #3 stands for me today. I'm making it. I can have good times. I've made new holidays or traditions. I do my job or my activities. I remember in the back of my mind, but the memories are okay, and do not interfere with my day. I can smile. I can feel in control, stronger, and able.

Stone #4 is a crystal in the rough. The roughness stands for the hard moments that may or may not come. It may be a hard panic feeling, or one of doubts, questions, anger, hurt, or fear. This rough rock is larger than the rest and feels so inside when it comes. When the rough times come, the rock tells me to go back to the beginning and look at my pouch and stones again. I will go back and read the steps again and help myself. I can also get help from others in my family, a counselor, a minister, rabbi, or others I can trust if I find that I feel really stuck. I can make it. I can hold on to my pouch, my memories and others . . . ALWAYS.

✳ ✳ ✳ ✳ ✳ ✳ ✳ ✳ ✳ ✳ ✳ ✳ ✳ ✳ ✳ ✳ ✳ ✳ ✳ ✳

CONFERENCE RITUALS

✳ ✳ ✳ ✳ ✳ ✳ ✳ ✳ ✳ ✳ ✳ ✳ ✳ ✳ ✳ ✳ ✳ ✳ ✳ ✳

NAME OF RITUAL
Healing Space Rituals

USED FOR
Camp Retreats and Conferences

APPROPRIATE AGES
Ten and up

LENGTH OF TIME
No defined time; this is done
when the individual is ready
to experience this throughout
the time of the conference
or camp

MATERIALS NEEDED
Long tables (about 6 ft.) put together in an alcove or separate
room; tables are covered with blue butcher paper and cedar
boughs are placed on them. Frequently colored plain paper is
placed on these tables, Native-American flute music or similar
natural sounding music is played on a tape recorder hidden in the
room. A Native-American basket of smooth black stones is placed
on one of the tables. Several explanatory messages about what to
do in this space is placed on the tables.

This ritual needs to be done at a conference or weekend activity
because of the need to have a separate space or room to allow for
the experience to be truly healing.

DESCRIPTION
Participants should be able to enter this "Healing Space" and be
transported to another place. The Healing Space symbolizes a
natural surrounding, hence the sense of blue water and cedar
boughs. Each participant is encouraged to take a piece of paper
and put a message to the deceased on it and then place it along
the blue "stream" where it will follow its natural path.
After completing the message, participants are invited to
take a stone with them to signify having visited this space
and having left something "to nature." Taking the stone is
nature's gift to the participant. The music and the quiet in this
space is very healing.

NAME OF RITUAL
Native-American Burden Basket

USED FOR
Camp and Conferences

APPROPRIATE AGES
Anyone old enough to write a
message or find something
special to place in the basket

LENGTH OF TIME
Any time is appropriate as this
is done individually

MATERIALS NEEDED
Native-American basket placed on a small table which is usually
covered with a Native-American blanket and some cedar boughs.
Optional: a picture of Mt. Rainier or some nearby mountain
peaks. Pieces of paper, pens, tissue. Frequently candles are used
to decorate the room.

DESCRIPTION
In 1989, a Native-American Shaman made a cedar Burden Basket
for the Seattle Chapter of The Compassionate Friends. Since that
time it has become a tradition to incorporate this ritual into all
Bereavement Services activities. The basket is medium sized and
because it is cedar it is "strong" enough to hold anger and tears.
Families are encouraged to enter the room where the basket is
kept (Reflection Room) and write a note, place a leaf or stone, put
a newspaper article, etc. into the basket. At the close of the
conference all the messages are taken to a Native American who
gives praise and blessing to these items, and then burns them. He
gathers the ashes together and then carries them up to the top of
Mt. Rainier where they are scattered and returned to Mother
Earth. This has been and continues to be a very powerful healing
tool, and of course no one knows what has been placed in the
basket, but it is clear that we are "rid" of the anger and pain and
more open to the healing. Lots of tears are shed in this room. This
can be a very helpful ritual.

****

UNIQUE TYPES
OF RITUALS

****

NAME OF RITUAL

Placing of Stones

USED FOR

Acknowledging a "visit" with the deceased, commonly done when visiting a Jewish cemetery; a pebble or stone is placed on top of the headstone following the visit to the grave.

APPROPRIATE AGES

Everyone/all people, adults and children are encouraged to do this

LENGTH OF TIME

The actual placing of the stone takes just a moment, however the visit to the cemetery is as long or short as desired.

MATERIALS NEEDED

All that is needed is a small pebble, usually found around the base of the grave

DESCRIPTION

Visitors take the stone and place it on top of the headstone or to the side of the monument when they have completed their time at the grave. The stone remains at the site acknowledging the visit to the deceased.

NAME OF RITUAL
Unveiling the Headstone

USED FOR
Jewish ritual approximately eleven months after the death; the headstone is mounted but kept covered during the months prior to the unveiling.

APPROPRIATE AGES
Participation is open to any age group. The ceremony is held at the cemetery.

LENGTH OF TIME
As short as ten minutes or as long as the family plans the ceremony

MATERIALS NEEDED
The stone is made during the year by monument workers and is mounted at the grave site. It is covered with cheesecloth. Invitations can be sent to family and friends prior to the event. A reception is frequently held at the home following the unveiling.

DESCRIPTION
The unveiling ceremony is usually preceded by appropriate prayers led by a rabbi or cantor. These are usually held in a circle around the grave, but in poor weather they can be held inside a chapel on the grounds of the cemetery. Following initial prayers there are frequently people asked to speak about the life of the deceased. Just prior to closing prayers or songs the cheesecloth is removed from the headstone by the closest relatives. Following the final prayers, as each person views the headstone and passes from the grave, a pebble is placed at the top of the headstone as an indication that the person has "visited" the deceased.

* * * * * * * * * * * * * * * * * * * *

POEMS
AND
MEDITATIONS

* * * * * * * * * * * * * * * * * * * *

ACKNOWLEDGMENTS

Many of the following poems, prayers and meditations have been com-
piled over the years from the following books and from other books read
in passing, but not remembered here:

A Leaf Touched the Sky

Gates of Prayer: The Reform Prayer Book

In the Midst of Winter

Kabbalet Shabbat, The Conservative Prayer Book

Seasonal Poems

The Eternal Light

The Holy Bible

The Mourner's Prayer Book

There is a Time for All Things

When Bad Things Happen to Good People

Wings of Prayer

Words of Our Fathers

All Must Answer the Summons

Early or Late, all must answer the summons to return to the Reservoir of Being. For we loose our hold on life when our time has come, as the leaf falls from the bough when its day is done. The deeds of the righteous enrich the world, as the fallen leaf enriches the soil beneath. The dust returns to the earth, the spirit lives on with God.

Like the stars by day, our beloved dead are not seen by mortal eyes. Yet they shine on forever, theirs is eternal peace.

Let us be thankful for the companionship that continues in a love stronger than death. Sanctifying the name of God, we do honor to their memory.

The Light of Life

The light of life is a finite flame. Like the candles we kindle, life is kindled, it burns, it glows, it is radiant with warmth and beauty. But soon it fades, its substance is consumed and it is no more.

In light we see; in light we are seen. The flames dance and our lives are full. But as night follows day, the candle of our life burns down and flutters. There is an end to the flames. We see no more and are no more seen. Yet we do not despair for we are more than a memory slowly fading into the darkness. With our lives we give life. Something of us can never die. We move in the eternal cycle of darkness and death, of light and life.

We Remember Them

In the rising of the sun and in its going down, we remember them.

In the blowing of the wind and in the chill of winter, we remember them.

In the opening of buds and in the rebirth of spring, we remember them.

In the blueness of the sky and in the warmth of summer, we remember them.

In the rustling of leaves and in the beauty of autumn, we remember them.

In the beginning of the year and when it ends, we remember them.

When we are weary and in need of strength, we remember them.

When we are lost and sick at heart, we remember them.

When we have joys we yearn to share, we remember them.

So long as we live, they too shall live, for they are now a part of us, as we remember them.

The Blessing of Memory

It is hard to sing of oneness when our world is not complete, when those who once brought wholeness to our life have gone, and naught but memory can fill the emptiness their passing leaves behind.

But memory can tell us only what we were, in company with those we loved; it cannot help us find what each of us, alone, must now become. Yet no one is really alone; those who live no more, echo still within our thoughts and words, and what they did is part of what we have become.

We do best homage to our dead when we live our lives most fully, even in the shadow of our loss. For each of our lives is worth the life of the whole world; in each one is the breath of the Ultimate One. In affirming the One, we affirm the worth of each one whose life, now ended, brought us closer to the Source of life, in whose unity no one is alone and every life finds purpose.

In Praise of Lives Now Gone

This the profound praise of the living.
  Praise for the generous gift of life.

Praise for the presence of loved ones,
  the bonds of friend
  the link of memory.

Praise for the toil and searching,
  the dedication and vision,
  the ennobling aspirations.

Praise for the precious moorings of faith.
  for the courageous souls
  for prophets, psalmists, and sages.

Praise for those who walked before us,
  the sufferers in the valley of shadows.
  the steadfast in the furnace of hate.

Praise for the God of our people,
  the Source of all growth and goodness
  the Promise on which we build tomorrow.

This is your time to weep and mourn, but sorrow is not forever. Even though it is difficult to believe this now, there will again be a time for you to smile and be at peace, a time to take up life once more.

For Everything there is a season and a time for every purpose under heaven:

A time to be born and a time to die:
  a time to plant and a time to uproot;

A time to kill and a time to heal;
  a time to break down and a time to build;

A time to weep and a time to laugh;
  a time to mourn and a time to dance;

A time to scatter stones and a time to gather them;
  a time to embrace and a time to refrain from embrace;

A time to seek and a time to lose;
  a time to keep and a time to cast away;

A time to tear and a time to mend;
  a time to be silent and a time to speak;

A time to love and a time to hate;
  a time for war and a time for peace.

In this sad world of ours, sorrow comes to all, and it often comes with bitter agony. Perfect relief is not possible except with time. You cannot now believe that you will ever feel better. But this is not true. You are sure to be happy again. Knowing this, truly believing it, will make you less miserable now. I have had enough experience to make this statement.

Abraham Lincoln

Twenty-Third Psalm

he Lord is my shepherd; I shall not want.

He maketh me to lie down in green pastures; he leadeth me beside the still waters.

He restoreth my soul: Yea though I walk through the valley of the shadow of death, I will fear no evil:
for thou art with me: thy rod and thy staff they comfort me.

Thou preparest a table before me in the presence of mine enemies: thou anointest my head with oil; my cup runneth over.

Surely goodness and mercy shall follow me all the days of my life:

and I will dwell in the house of the Lord forever.

God of life, there are days when the burdens
we carry chafe our shoulders and wear us down;
when the road seems dreary and endless, the
skies grey and threatening; when our lives
have no music in them, and our hearts are lonely,
and our souls have lost their courage.
Flood the path with light, we beseech Thee;
turn our eyes to where the skies are full of promise . . .

Augustine

What we have once enjoyed
we can never lose

All that we love deeply
becomes a part of us.

Helen Keller

Meditation

Oh God of life, amid the ceaseless tides of change which sweep away the generations, Your loving spirit remains to comfort us and give us hope. Around us is life and death, decay and renewal; the flowing rhythm that all things obey.

Our life is a dance to a song we cannot hear. Its melody courses through us for a little while, then seems to cease. Whence the melody, and whither does it go? In darkness as in light, we turn to You, Lord, the Source of life, the Answer to all its mysteries.

Can it be that we, Your children, are given over to destruction, when our few days on earth are done? Or do we live in ways we cannot know?

Only this have we been taught, and in this we put our trust: from You comes the spirit, and to You it must return. You are our dwelling place in life and in death.

More we cannot say, for all else is hidden from our sight by an impenetrable veil. We thank You, then, for the life we have, and for the gifts that daily are our portion:

For health and healing, for labor and repose, for the ever-renewed beauty of earth and sky, for thoughts of truth and justice that move us to acts of goodness, and for the contemplation of Your eternal Presence, which fills us with the hope that what is good and lovely will not perish.

After a Tragic Loss

 God, help me to live with my grief!

Death has taken my beloved, and I feel that I cannot go on. My faith is shaken; my mind keeps asking: Why? Why does joy end in sorrow? Why does love exact its price in tears? Why?

O God, help me to live with my grief!

Help me to accept the mystery of life. Help me to see that even if my questions were answered, even if I did know why, the pain would be no less, the loneliness would remain bitter beyond words. Still my heart would ache.

O God, help me to triumph over my grief!

Help me to endure this night of anguish. Help me to walk through the darkness with faith in tomorrow. Give me comfort, give me courage, turn me to deeds that bless the living.

O God, help me to triumph over my grief.

A Philosophy

Judaism teaches us to understand death as part of the Divine pattern of the universe. Actually, we could not have our sensitivity without fragility. Mortality is the tax that we pay for the privilege of love, thought, creative work—the toll on the bridge of being from which clods of earth and snow-peaked mountain summits are exempt. Just because we are human, we are prisoners of the years, yet that very prison is the room of discipline in which we, driven by the urgency of time, create.

How Can We Understand Death?

What can we know of death, we who cannot understand life?

We study the seed and the cell, but the power deep within them will always elude us.

Though we cannot understand, we accept life as the gift of God. Yet death, life's twin, we face with fear.

But why be afraid? Death is a haven to the weary, a relief for the sorely afflicted. We are safe in death as in life.

There is no pain. There is only the pain of the living as they recall shared loves, and as they themselves fear to die.

Calm us, O Lord, when we cry out in our fear and our grief. Turn us anew toward life and the world. Awaken us to the warmth of human love that speaks to us of You.

We shall fear no evil as we affirm Your kingdom of life.

A Butterfly

A Butterfly Lights Beside Us
    Like a Sunbeam.
And for a Brief Moment
    Its Glory and Beauty
Belong to our World.

But then it Flies on Again
    And Though We Wish
        It Could Have Stayed
We Feel Lucky To Have Seen It.

LINKS

The links of life are broken,
but the links of love and longing never break.

The best and most beautiful things in the world cannot be
seen or even touched. They must be felt with the heart.

Come let us walk among the distant stars . . . there are no gates—
no fences—and no bars. Out there among the stars we
    will be free . . . there are no shadows for the heart to see.

Could spring's fresh beauty lift your heart as high
    had not dark branches touched the winter sky—

Grief only becomes a tolerable and creative experience
when love enables it to be shared with someone who really
understands.

Winston O. Abbott
Simon Stephens

When darkness seems overwhelming,
light a candle in someone's life and see
how it makes the darkness in your own
and the other person's life flee.

Rabbi Harold Kushner

EAUTIFUL

PEOPLE

DO

NOT

JUST

HAPPEN . . .

out of the depths

of defeat, suffering,

struggle and loss comes

an appreciation, sensitivity

and an understanding of life filled with

compassion, gentleness, and
a deep loving concern.

The melody that our loved one played upon the piano of our lives will never be played quite that way again, but we must not close the keyboard and allow the instrument to gather dust. We must seek out other artists of the spirit; new friends who gradually will help us to find the road of life again, who will walk that road with us.

Rabbi Joshua Liebman

A Sanskrit Proverb

Look to this day, for it is life.
For yesterday is already a dream
and tomorrow is only a vision.

But today well lived makes
every yesterday
a dream of happiness, and
every tomorrow
a vision of hope.

PLACES I REMEMBER

There are places I remember
All my life, though some have changed
Some forever, not for better
Some are gone
And some remain.

All these places have their moments
Wither lovers and friends, I still can recall
Some are dead
And some are living
In my life, I've loved them all.

But of all these friends and lovers
There is no one compares with you
And these memories lose their meaning
When I think of love as something new.

You know I'll often stop and think about them
These places and friends that went before.
Yes, I'll often stop and think about them
But in my life, I've loved you more.

O God Our Help

O God, our help in ages past, our hope for years to come.
Our shelter from the stormy blast, and our eternal home.

Before the hills in order stood, or earth received her frame.
From everlasting You are God, to endless years the same.

Beneath the shadow of Your throne, Your children dwell secure
Sufficient is Your arm alone, and our defence is sure.

O God, our help in ages past, our hope for years to come,
Be now our guide while troubles last, and our eternal home.

Psalm 121

I lift up my eyes to the mountains, what is the source of my help?

My help will come from the Lord, Maker of heaven and earth.

He will not allow your foot to slip;

your Guardian will not slumber.

Behold, the Guardian of Israel neither slumbers nor sleeps.

the Eternal is your Keeper, the Lord is your shade at your right hand.

The sun shall not harm you by day, not the moon by night. The Lord will guard you from all evil. He will protect your being.

The Lord will guard you, coming and going, from this time forth, and for ever.

In Recent Grief

When cherished ties are broken, and the chain of love is shattered, only trust and the strength of faith can lighten the heaviness of the heart. At times, the pain of separation seems more than we can bear, but if we dwell too long on our loss we embitter our hearts and harm ourselves and those about us.

The Psalmist said that in his affliction he learned the law of God. And in truth, grief is a great teacher, when it sends us back to serve and bless the living. We learn how to counsel and comfort those who, like ourselves, are bowed with sorrow. We learn when to keep silence in their presence and when a word will assure them of our love and concern.

Thus, even when they are gone, the departed are with us, moving us to live as, in their higher moments, they themselves wished to live. We remember them now, they live in our hearts; they are an abiding blessing.

Meditation

As in the world around us, so too in human life, darkness is followed by light and sorrow by comfort. Life and death are twins; grief and hope walk hand in hand. Although we cannot know what lies beyond the body's death, let us put our trust in the undying Spirit who calls us into life and who abides to all eternity.

O Lord, God of the spirits of all flesh, You are close to the hearts of the sorrowing, to strengthen and console them with the warmth of Your love, and with the assurance that the human spirit is enduring and indestructible. Even as we pray for perfect peace for those whose lives have ended, so do we ask You to give comfort and courage to the living.

May the knowledge of Your nearness be our strength, O God, for You are with us at all times: in joy and sorrow, in light and darkness, in life and death.

O God, full of compassion, Eternal Spirit of the universe, grant perfect rest under the wings of Your Presence to our loved one who has entered eternity. Master of Mercy, let him (her) find refuge forever in the shadow of Your wings and let his (her) soul be bound up in the bond of eternal life. The Eternal God is his (her) inheritance. May he (she) rest in peace, and let us say Amen.

O Lord, Healer of the broken-hearted and Binder of their wounds, grant consolation to those who mourn. Give them strength and courage in the time of their grief, and restore to them a sense of life's goodness.

Fill them with reverence and love for You, that they may serve You with a whole heart, and let them soon know peace.

BIBLIOGRAPHY OF BOOKS
RELATED TO RITUALS

Abbott, Winston, *Come Walk among the Stars,* South Windsor: Inspiration House, 1966.

Acterberg, Jeanne, *Rituals of Healing,* New York: Bantam Books, 1989.

Ardinger, Barbara, *A Woman's Book of Rituals and Celebrations,* New York: New World Library, 1995.

Bali, *Further Studies in Life, Thought, and Ritual,* Amsterdam: Van Hoeve, 1969.

Bierhorst, John, *In the Trail of the Wind: American Indian Poems and Rituals,* New York: Farrar, Straus, 1971.

Burrell, Percy Jewett, *Watchers of the World, A Dramatic Ritual in Honor of the Living,* New York: Baker's Plays, 1944.

Byne, David, *Strange Ritual: Pictures and Words,* Chicago: Chronicle Books, 1995.

Cahill, Sedonia, *The Ceremonial Circle: Practice, Ritual and Renewal,* San Francisco: Harper Collins, 1992.

Capacchione, Lucia, *The Picture of Health,* Santa Monica: Hay House, 1990.

Childs-Growell, Elaine, *Good Grief Rituals: Tools for Healing,* Station Hill Press, 1992.

Cohen, B. M., Barnes, M., Rankin, A. B., *Managing Traumatic Stress through Art: Drawing from the Center,* Lutherville, Maryland: The Sidran Press, 1995.

Cole, D., *After Great Pain: A New Life Emerges,* New York: Summit Books, 1992.

Dobrinski, Conrad, *A Muse for the Masses: Ritual and Music in an Age of Democratic Policies,* Chicago: University of Chicago, 1977.

Dobrinsky, Herbert, *A Treasury of Sephardic Laws and Customs: The Ritual Practices,* New York: Ktav Yeshiva University, 1986.

Doka, Kenneth, *Disenfranchised Grief,* Lexington, Massachusetts: Lexington Books, 1989.

Donelly, Katherine Fair, *Recovering from the Loss of a Sibling,* New York: Dodd, Mead and Co., 1988.

Driver, Tom Faw, *The Magic of Ritual: Our Need for Liberating Rites that Transform,* San Francisco: Harper Collins, 1991.

Ernst, Alive, *The Wolf Ritual of the Northwest Coast,* Eugene, University of Oregon, 1952.

Feinstein, David, *Personal Mythology: The Psychology of Your Evolving Self,* New York: Tarcher, Inc., 1988.

Fulghum, Robert, *From Beginning to End: The Rituals of Our Lives,* New York: Villard Books, 1995.

Gillis, John, *A World of Their Own Making: Myth, Ritual and the Quest,* Boston: Basic Books, 1996.

Glass-Koentop, Pattalee, *Year of Moons, Season of Threes,* Boston: Llewellyn Publications, 1991.

Gootman, Marilyn, *When a Friend Dies,* Minneapolis: Free Spirit, 1994.

Hammerschlag, Carl A., *The Thief of the Spirit: Journey to Spiritual Healing,* New York: Simon and Schuster, 1993.

Harrison, Jane, *Ancient Art and Ritual,* New York: H. Holt and Co., 1913.

Heffernan, William, *Ritual,* New York: New American Library, 1988.

Highwater, Jamake, *Ritual of the Wind: North American Indian Ceremonies,* New York: Viking Press, 1977.

Hirschfield, Jane, *Women in Praise of the Sacred,* New York: Harper Collins, 1994.

Huet, Michael, *The Dance, Art and Ritual of Africa,* New York: Pantheon Books, 1978.

Huntington, Richard, *Celebrations of Death: The Anthropology of Mortuary Ritual,* Oxford: Cambridge University, 1979.

Imber-Black, Evan, *Rituals for Our Times: Celebrating, Healing and Changing Our Lifes,* New York: Harper Collins, 1992.

James, Edwin, *Christian Myth and Ritual: A Historical Study,* Meridian Books, 1965.

Kertzer, David, *Ritual, Politics, and Power,* New Haven: Yale University Press, 1988.

Metrick, S. B., *Crossing the Bridge: Creating Ceremonies for Grieving and Healing from Life's Losses,* Berkeley: Celestial Arts, 1994.

Moffat, Mary Jane, *In the Midst of Winter—Selections from the Literature of Mourning,* New York: Vantage Press, 1982.

Morgan, E., *Dealing Creatively with Death: A Manual of Death Education and Simple Burial,* Burnsville, North Carolina: Celo Press, 1984.

Morgan, John, *Young People and Death,* Philadelphia: Charles Press, 1991.

Morgenson, G., *Greeting the Angels: An Imaginal View of the Mourning Process,* Amityville, New York: Baywood Publishing Co., 1995.

Nelson, Gertrud, *To Dance with God: Family Ritual and Community Celebration,* Paulist Press, 1986.

Radin, Paul, *The Road of Life and Death, a Ritual Drama of the American Indian,* New York: Pantheon Books, 1945.

Roberts, Janice and Joy Johnson, *Thank You for Coming to Say Good-Bye,* Omaha: Centering Corp., 1994.

Rushton, Lucy, *Death Customs,* Cincinnati: Thomason Learning, 1993.

Schechner, Richard, *The Future of Ritual: Writings on Culture and Performance,* New York: Routledge, 1993.

Scheff, Thomas, *Catharsis in Healing, Ritual and Drama,* Los Angeles: University of California, 1979.

Scruggs, Anderson, *Ritual for Myself,* New York: Macmillan Publishing, 1941.

Seward, Jack, *Hara-Kiri: Japanese Ritual Suicide,* C. E. Tuttle, 1968.

Shelemay, Kay, *Music, Ritual and Falasha History,* Lancing: Michigan State University, 1989.

Silverman, Morris, *Prayers of Consolation,* New York: Prayer Book Press, 1953.

Some, Malidoma, *Ritual: Power, Healing and Community,* Swan/Raven Press, 1993.

Stein, Diane, *Casting the Circle: A Women's Book of Rituals,* Crossing Press, 1990.

Strocchia, Sharon, *Death and Ritual in Renaissance Florence,* Baltimore: Johns Hopkins University Press, 1992.

Strocchia, Sharon, *Death Ritual in Late Imperial and Modern China,* Los Angeles: University of California, 1988.

Watts, Alan, *Myth and Ritual in Christianity,* New York: Vanguard Press, 1953.

Webb, Nancy Boyd, *Helping Bereaved Children,* New York: Guilford Press, 1993.

Zunin, Lenard and Hilary, *The Art of Condolence,* New York: Harper Collins, 1991.

About the Editor

ANN MARIE PUTTER

Ann Marie Putter received her education at the University of Southern California majoring in music and psychology. She is a Certified Mental Health Counselor and a Certified Grief Counselor with specialization in Pediatric Bereavement. She is also a Music Therapist. Ann Marie was founder and director of the *Children Grieve, Too* program for Family Services in Seattle, Washington for eight years, and has presented workshops throughout the United States and Canada on children's grief issues. Ann Marie was the chairperson of the first *World Gathering on Bereavement* and has chaired many conferences and retreats for bereaved families. Ann Marie currently works in Employee Assistance at Family Services and serves as an expert witness on parental bereavement for the Superior and Appellate Courts of Washington. She previously co-wrote *"Shira, a Legacy of Courage"* by Sharon Grollman, 1988, and *"Saying Goodbye . . . A Children's Grief Kit"* with Ellen Zahlis, 1991. Ann Marie lives with her husband and son in Newcastle, Washington.